Last year you had your ups and downs.
Lets smile for the blessings and no more frowns.
Lets celebrate the wins and the losses.
Lets come together and create more bosses.
If you change your mindset you will win.
Just know the competition is within.
Let go of grudges and learn from the past.
Start creating memories with love ones that will last.
Just know what is meant to be will be.
Happy New Mindset from Miss Dejha B!

Cheers to your new Mindset!

Dejha B

New Year New Mindset

© 2021 by Dejha B. All rights reserved.

First Published in the United States of America in 2021
by Black Angel Publishing.

First Printing, 2021

No part of this book may be reproduced in any manner whatsoever
without written permission of the author, Dejha B or the publisher,
Black Angel Publishing except for use of brief quotations in a book review.

ISBN-978-1-7359976-2-9

Created and Conceptualized by Dejha B

Illustrations by: Dejha B & Samiramakroum

Editors: Dolores Brunner and Nia Imani Davis

For more coloring books visit:
www.dejhabcoloring.com

Vision Board

This New Year and New Mindset Belongs To:

Establish Healthy Sleeping Habits!

1. Keep an consistent sleep schedule.
2. Establish a relaxing bedtime routine.
3. Make your bedroom quiet and relaxing.
4. Turn off electronics at least 30 minutes before bedtime.
5. Set a bedtime early enough for you to get 7 hours of sleep.

Get More Organized.

1. Buy a planner.
2. Write things down.
3. De-clutter regularly.
4. Make schedules and deadlines.

Start Expressing Yourself Artistically

1. Take a painting class.
2. Color More.
3 Write Music.
4. Learn to play an instrument.
5. Take a photography class.

Stop Being Late All The Time!

1. Get your stuff ready the night before.
2. Give yourself time for traffic/delays.
3. Set your alarm.

What Will You Commit Yourself To?

Live Debt Free!

Volunteer More.

1. Visit a senior center.
2. Tutor a student.
3. Provide mentorship.
4. Fix and serve meals.

Earn And Save More Money.

1. You should have at least 7 streams of income!
2. You should save at least 20% of your income.

I Am Eating Healthier!

1. Try new smoothie recipes.
2. Limit high processed food.
3. Drink more water.

I Am Exercising More!

1. Make a schedule.
2 Start gradually.
3. Find motivation.
4. Track your progress.
5. Give yourself a reward.

Sis Stop Going Back To Your Ex!

Let Go Of Grudges.

1. Write a letter towards the person you have a grudge towards.
2. Express how they hurt you in the letter.
3. Read it out loud.
4. Forgive them
4. Throw it away.
5. Release that energy, and regain your power.

Learn A New Language!

Learn From The Past!

1. Reflect on it.
2. Study It.
3. Learn the lesson.
4. Release yourself from it.
5. Use the lesson.

I Will Read More!

1. List some books you will read this year.

READ READ

READ READ

READ READ

READ READ

Let Your "No" Mean "No"!

1. Saying no helps you establish healthy boundaries.
2. Saying no is empowering.

Become More Social!

1. Hang out with some like-minded people.
2. Have a girls night out with your friends.
3. Go to networking events.

Stand Up For Yourself!

1. Say what you mean, and mean what you say!

Set Boundaries!

Travel More!

1. List some places you want to visit.

Turn Your Hobby Into A Business!

Start Writing In Your Journal!

1. Writing improves memory.
2. Journaling has similar benefits to meditation.
3. Inspires creativity.
4. Relieve stress.
5. Set and achieve goals.

Selfcare Is the Best Care!

DON'T LET YOUR HUSTLE COME BEFORE YOUR HEALTH

Spend More Time With People That Matter!

1. Plan ahead.
2. Have a least one meal together.
3. Plan a day out each month.
4. Cook a meal together.
5. Plan a fun activity together at least 1 hour a week.

Establish Priorities.

1. Make prioritized task list for the day.
2. Focus on your most important task.
3. Be flexible.
4. Plan ahead.

Spend Less Time On Social Media!

Be More Responsible!

1. Stop making excuses for yourself.
2. Be consistent.
3. Avoid procrastination.

Face Your Fears!

1. Relax and be Calm.
2. Talk about it.
3. Evaluate Risk.
4. Create an action plan.
5. Take small steps.

Reduce Stress!

1. Color more to reduce stress.
2. Try meditating every morning.
3. Don't sweat the small stuff.

Reinvent Yourself!

Word Search:

1. Find the words that will be apart of your new year.

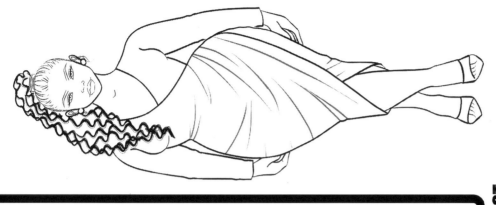
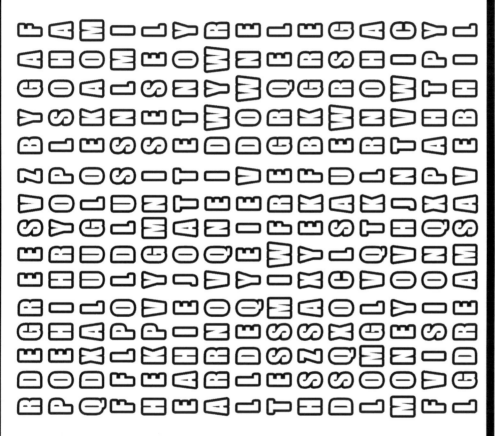

```
R D E G R E E S V Z B Y G A F
P O E H I H R V O P L S O H A
Q D X A L U G L O E K A O M I
F F L P O L D U S N L M I E L
H E K P V G M N I S E S E T V
E A H I E J O A T T E T N O Y
A R R N O V Q N E I E V D W R
L L D E Q Y E I E V D O W N E
T E S S M I W F R E G B Q E L
H S Z S A X Y E K F B K G R E
D S Q X O C L S A U E W R S G
L O M G L V Q T K L R N O H A
M O N E Y O V H J N T W I C
F V I S I O N Q X P A H T P Y
L G D R E A M S A V E B H I L
```

HOMEOWNERSHIP · **VOLUNTEER** · **HAPPINESS** · **MANIFEST**
POSITIVE · **FEARLESS** · **DEGREES** · **NETWORK**
HEALTH · **DREAMS** · **WEALTH** · **LEGACY**
MONEY · **FAMILY** · **VISION** · **GOALS**
SAVE · **BLESSED** · **GROWTH** · **LOVE**

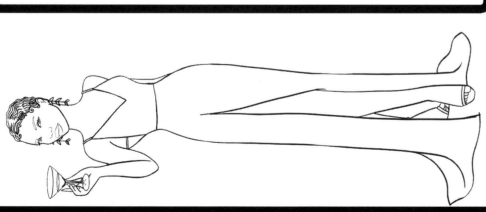

Spend Less Time Watching TV.

New Year New Mindset

I hope you have a wonderful year.

For more coloring books visit
www.dejhabcoloring.com

Please Follow the brand "Dejha B Coloring" social media pages:

Instagram and Facebook pages @DejhaBColoring and tag your coloring pages.
Use Hashtag #DejhaBColoring

Please join "DejhaBColoring" Facebook Group to share your coloring pages.

Please follow "Black Angel Publishing" social media pages for more Inspirational books

Instagram: @BlackAngelPublishing
Facebook Page: www.facebook.com/BlackAngelPublishing

Follow the Creator/Author Dejha B
Instagram: @iamdejhab2
www.iamdejhab.com
Facebook Page: www.facebook.com/iamdejhab2

New Year NEW Mindset

Test Your Coloring Tools On This Page

amy@fastpatterns.com
please send me proof